Silly Animal Facts

HANDWRITING WORKBOOK

This book belongs to

_____
- - - - - - - - - - - - - - - - - -
_____
- - - - - - - - - - - - - - - - - -
_____

Copyright 2023
www.clawandson.com
www.facebook.com/clawandson

Introduction

Step into the wonderfully wacky world of silly animal facts! This book is not just about handwriting perfection; it's also an exploration of information that makes studying enticingly enjoyable. We understand that when learning material sparks genuine interest, like these fascinating facts, kids remain focused and engaged.

Before the silly animal facts, the first set of pages start with the alphabet where letters are practiced through tracing. Each letter is presented with directional arrows to show the hand movements as kids learn to improve their handwriting and fine motor skills.

As your child stands on the brink of a fact learning adventure in handwriting, please note that this book has been thoughtfully designed with minimal distractions to help young learners stay focused on mastering simple sentences. The path to neat, legible handwriting is paved with patience and practice, and it's our hope that the engaging content within these pages will make that journey both entertaining and effective.

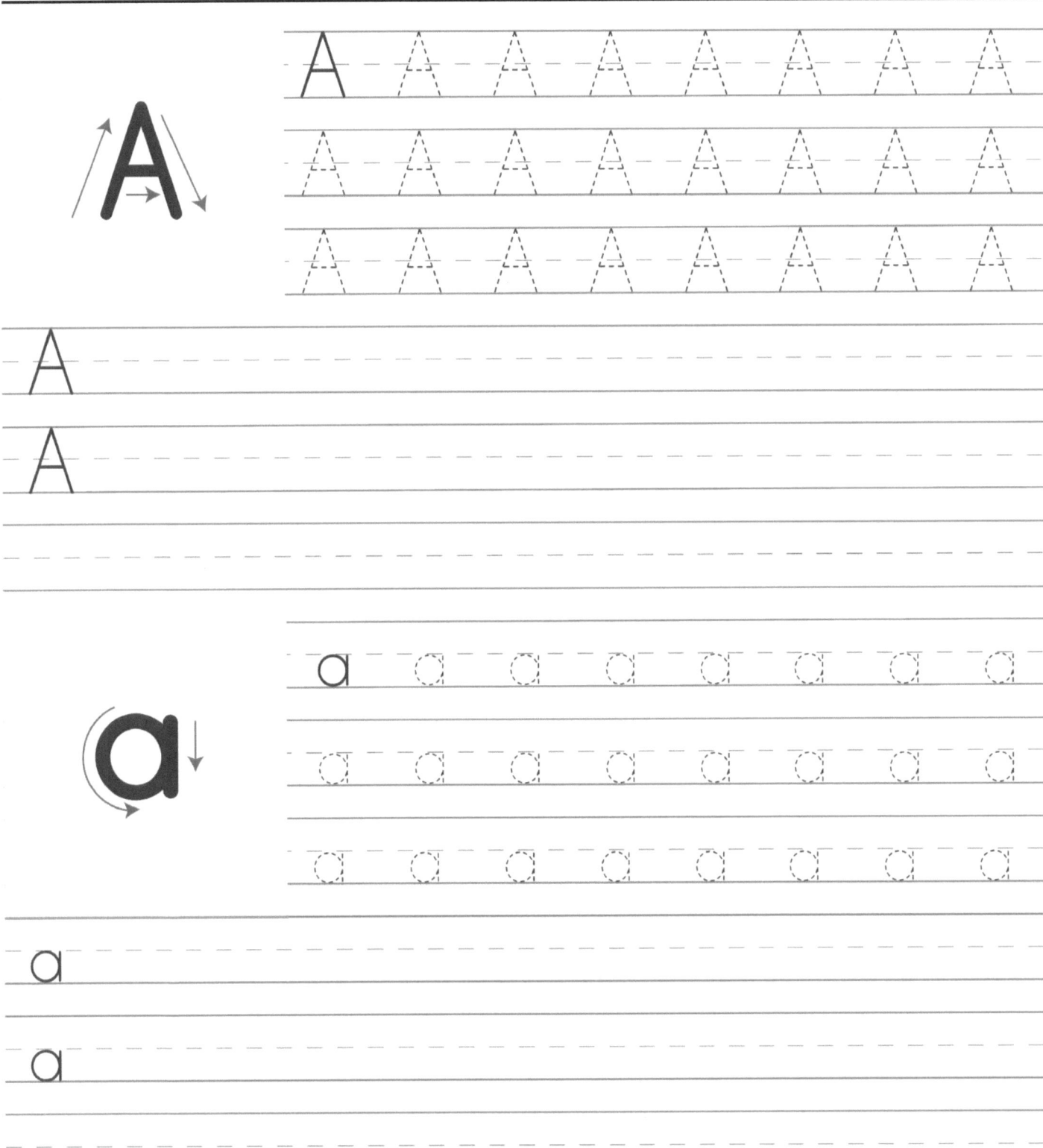

Bb

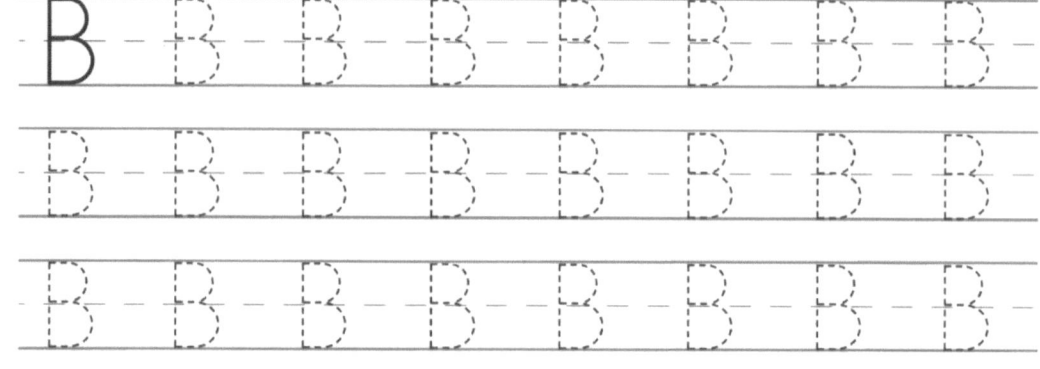

B

B

b

b

Cc

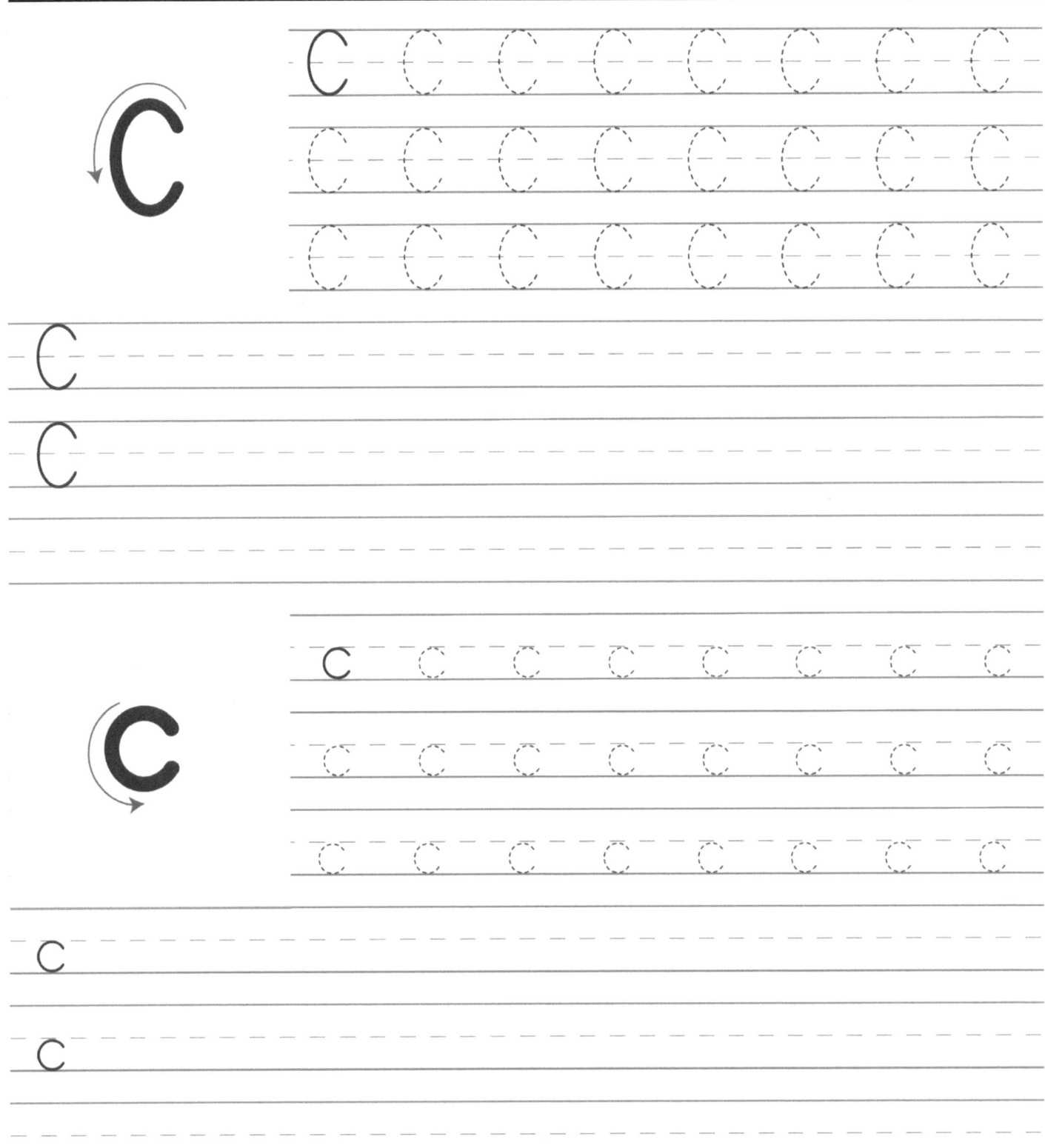

Dd

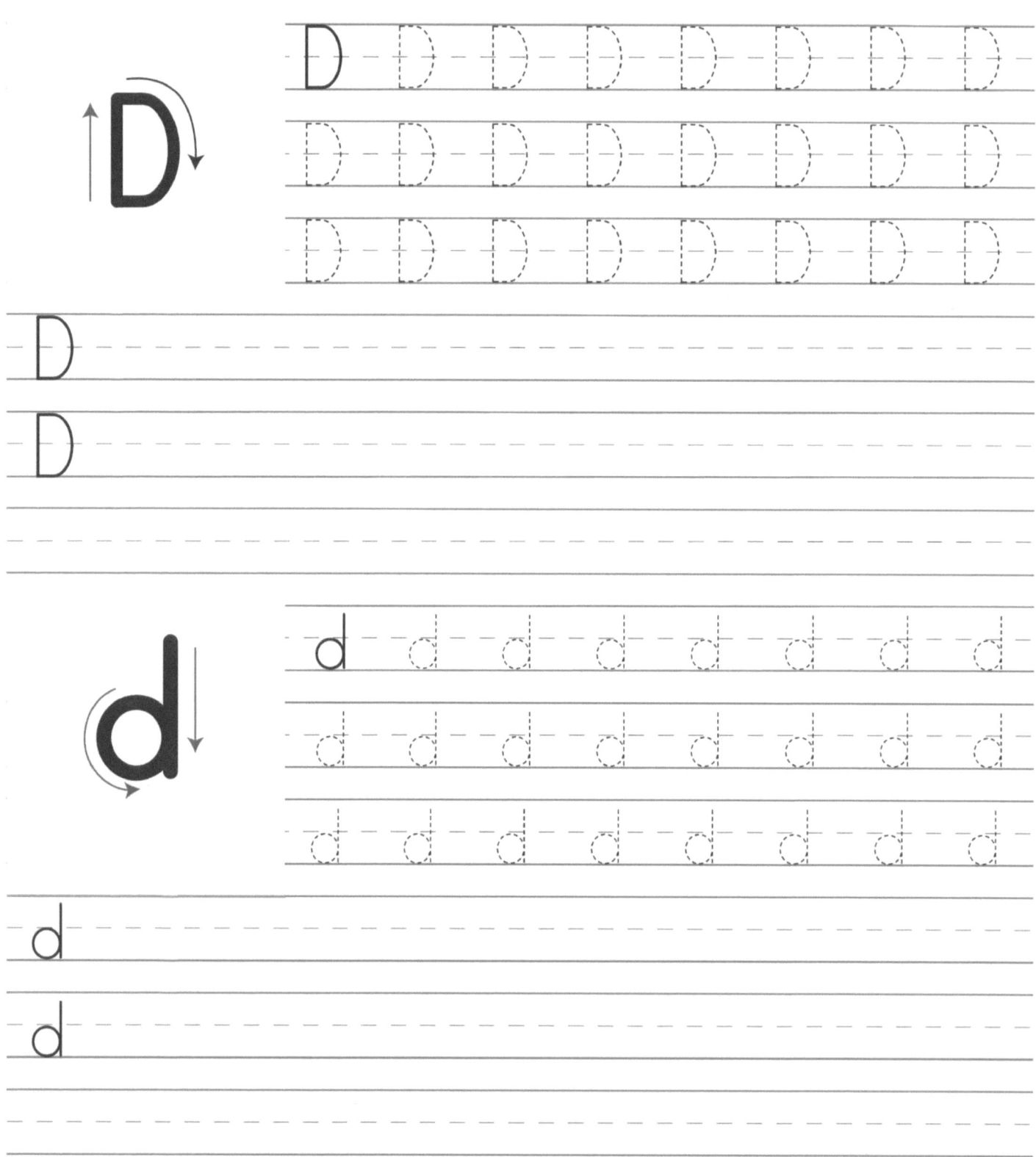

Ee

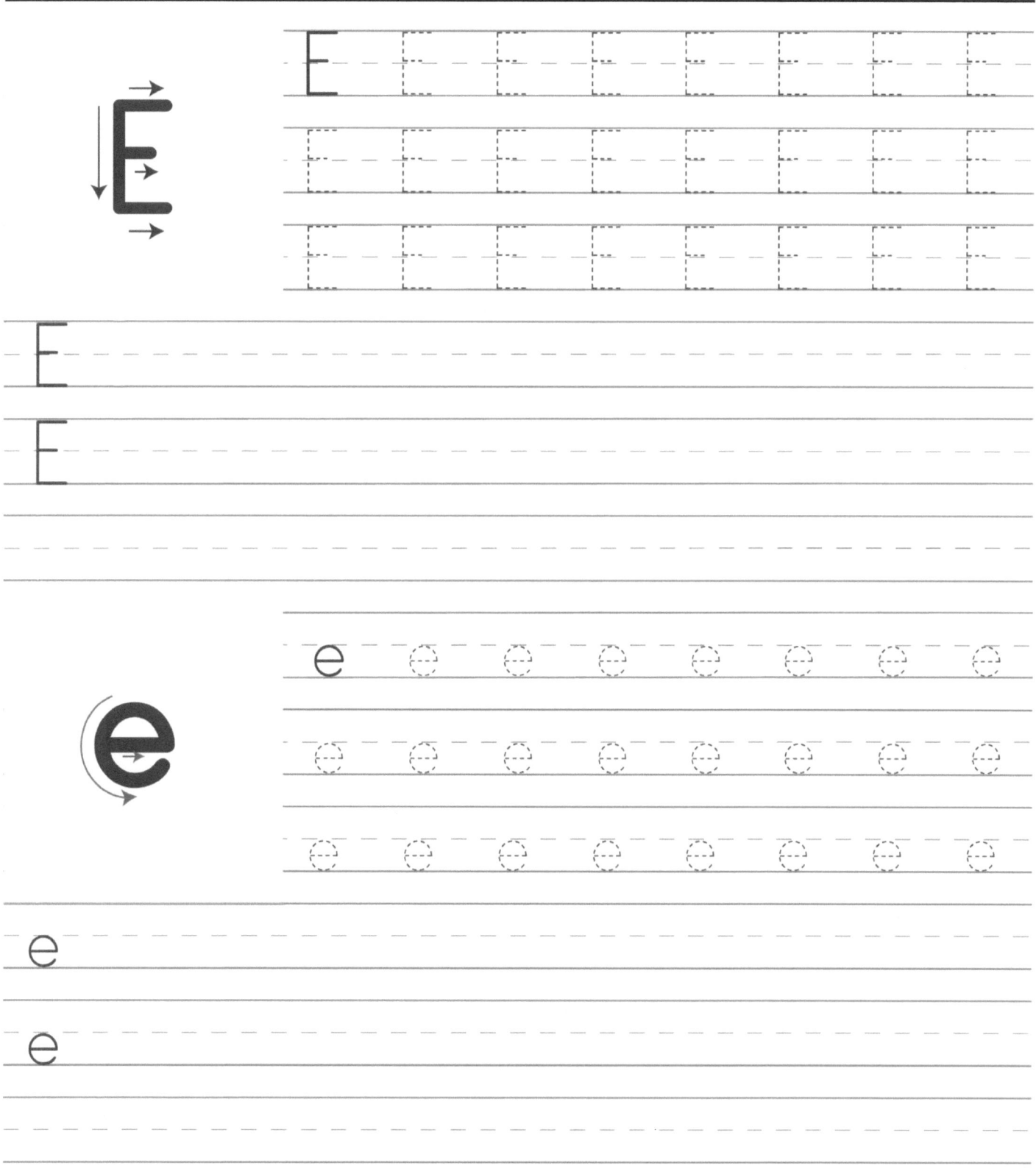

F f

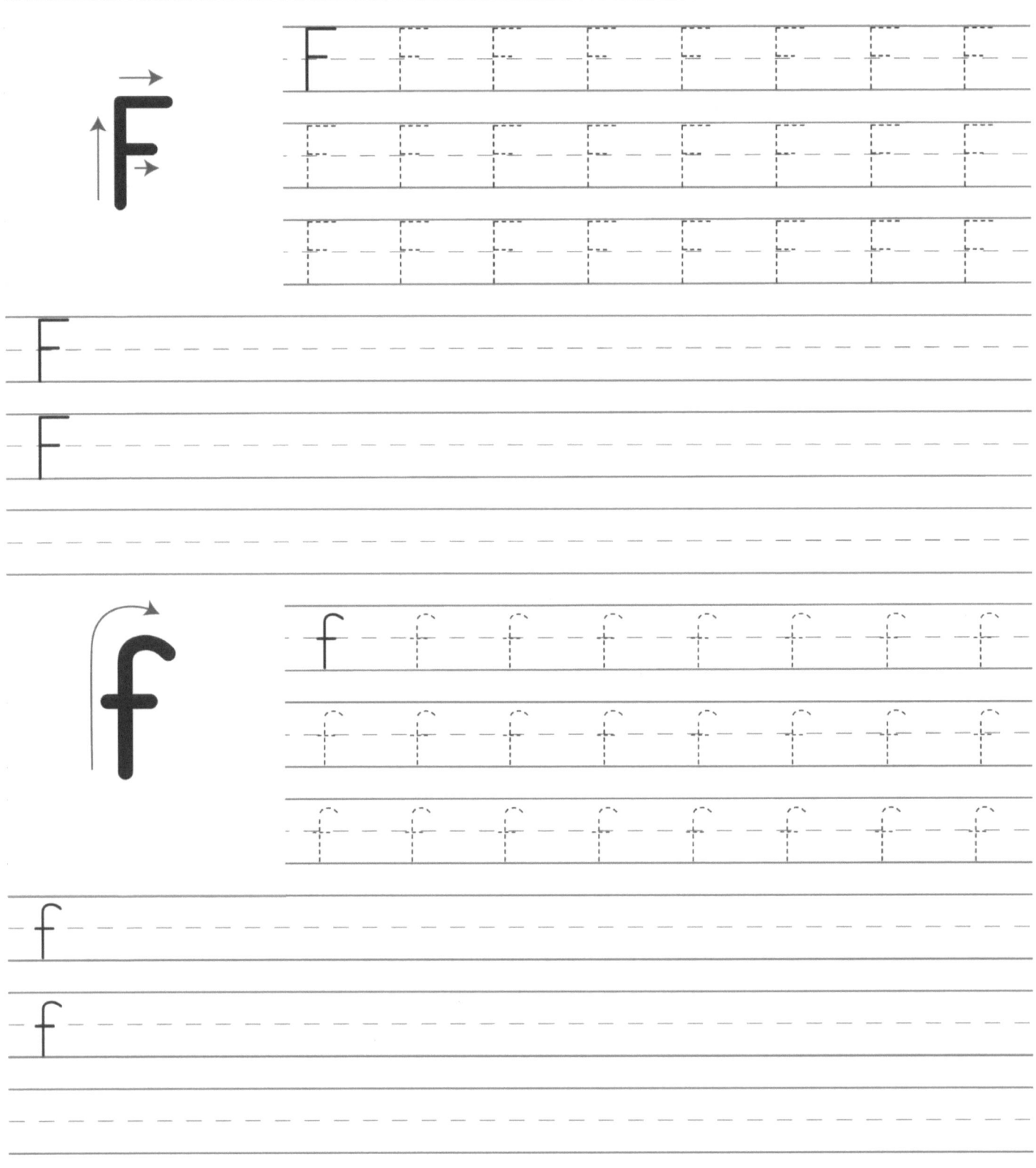

Gg

G

G G G G G G G G

G G G G G G G G

G G G G G G G G

G

G

g

g g g g g g g g

g g g g g g g g

g g g g g g g g

g

g

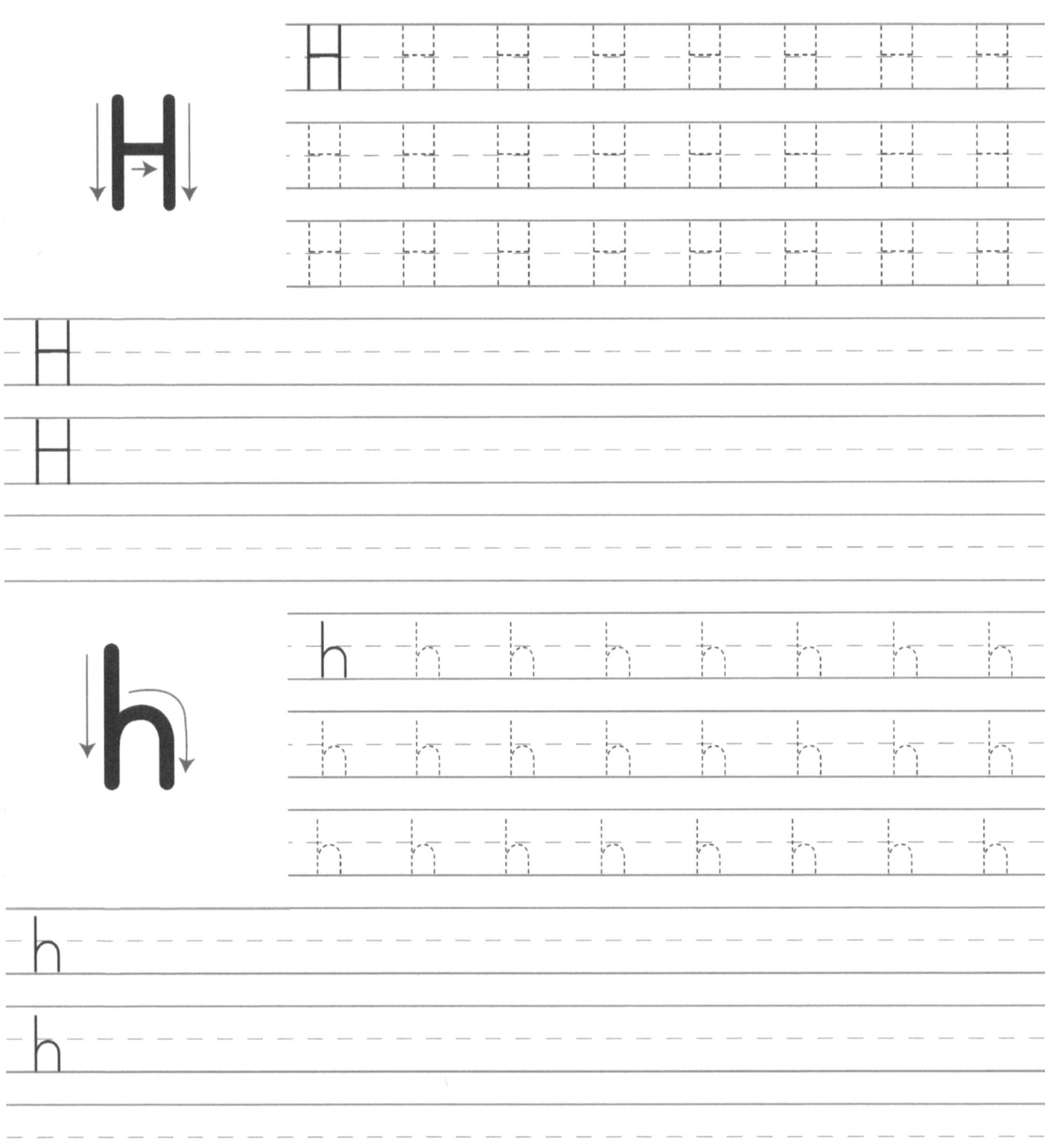

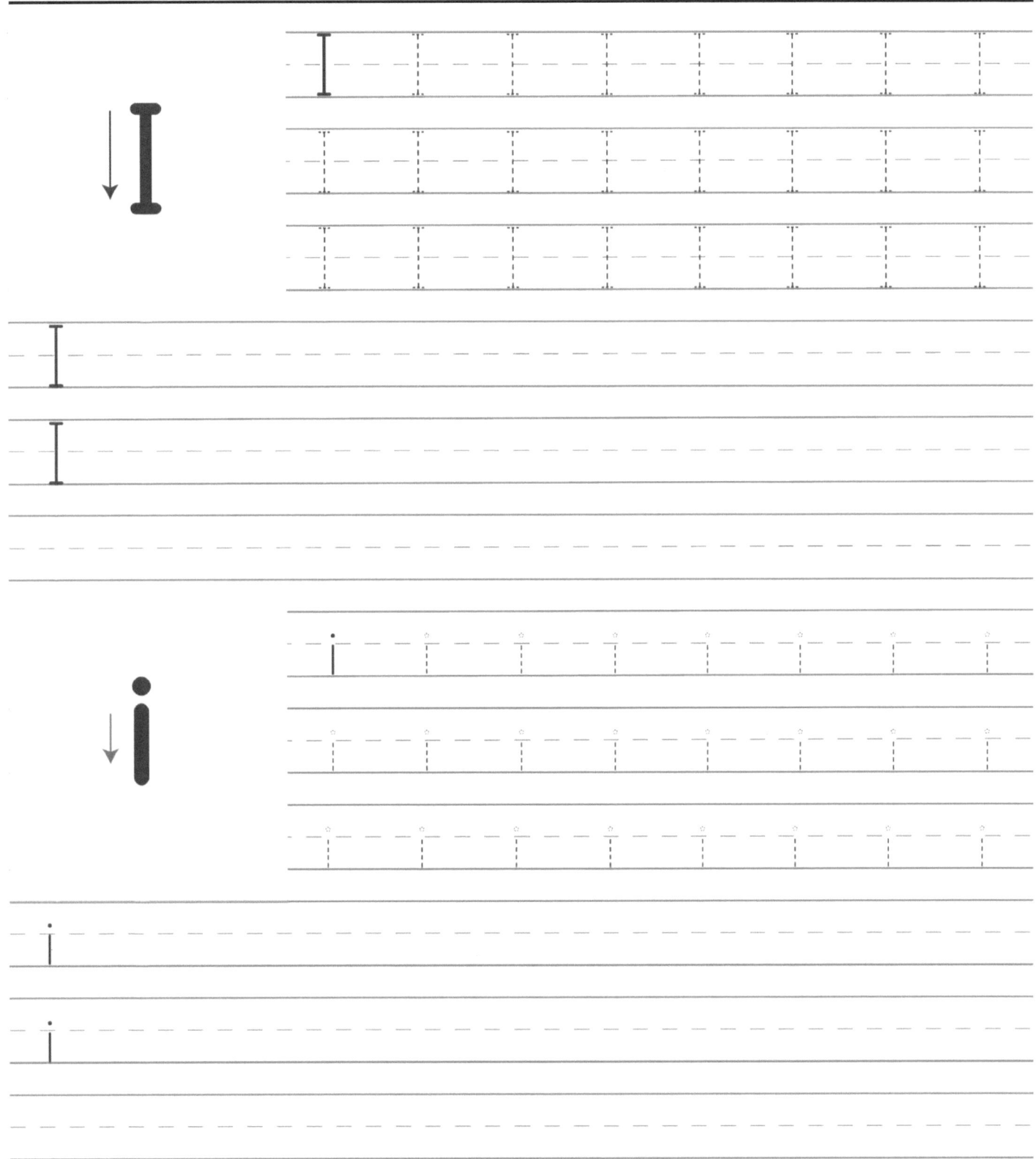

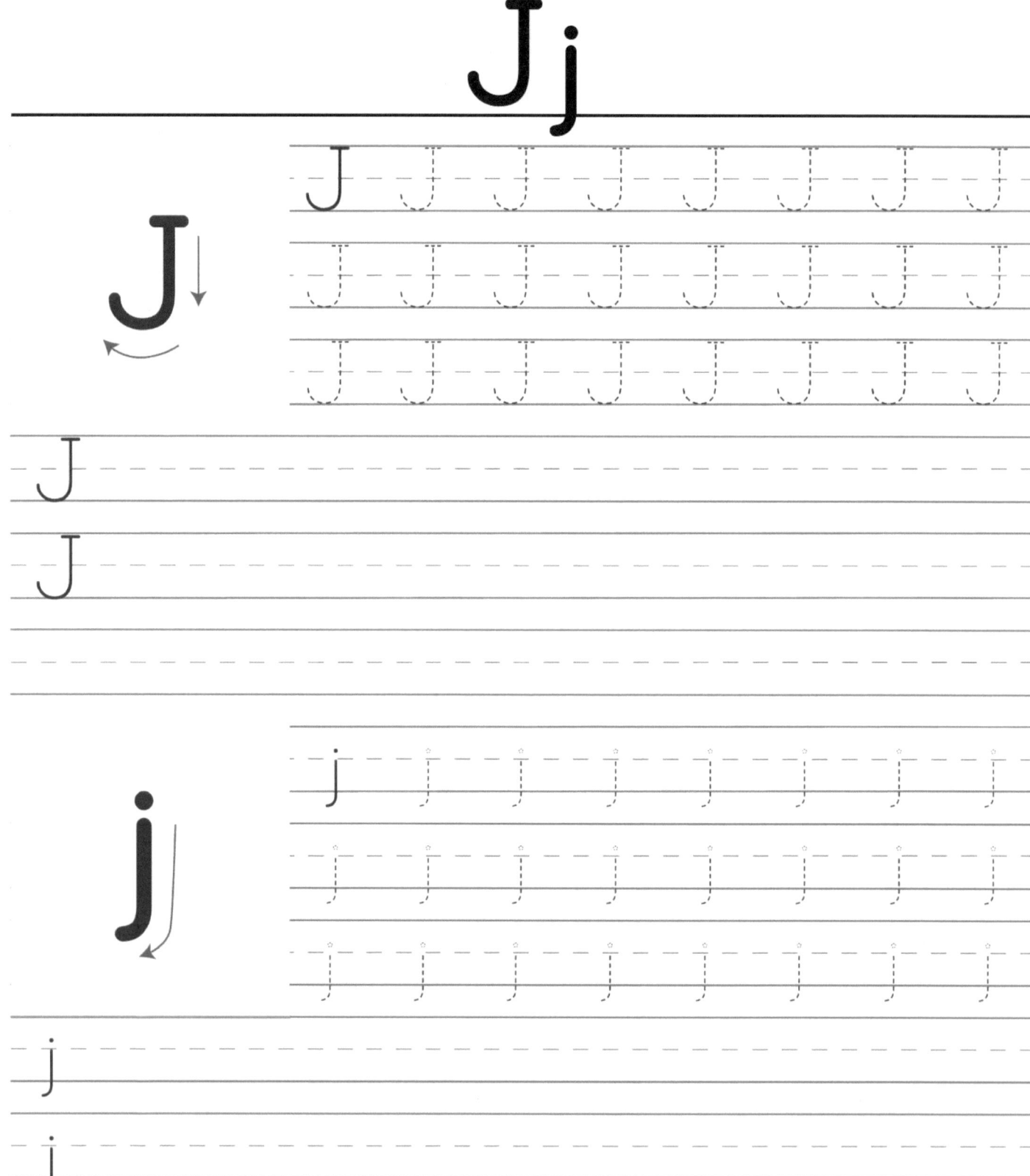

Kk

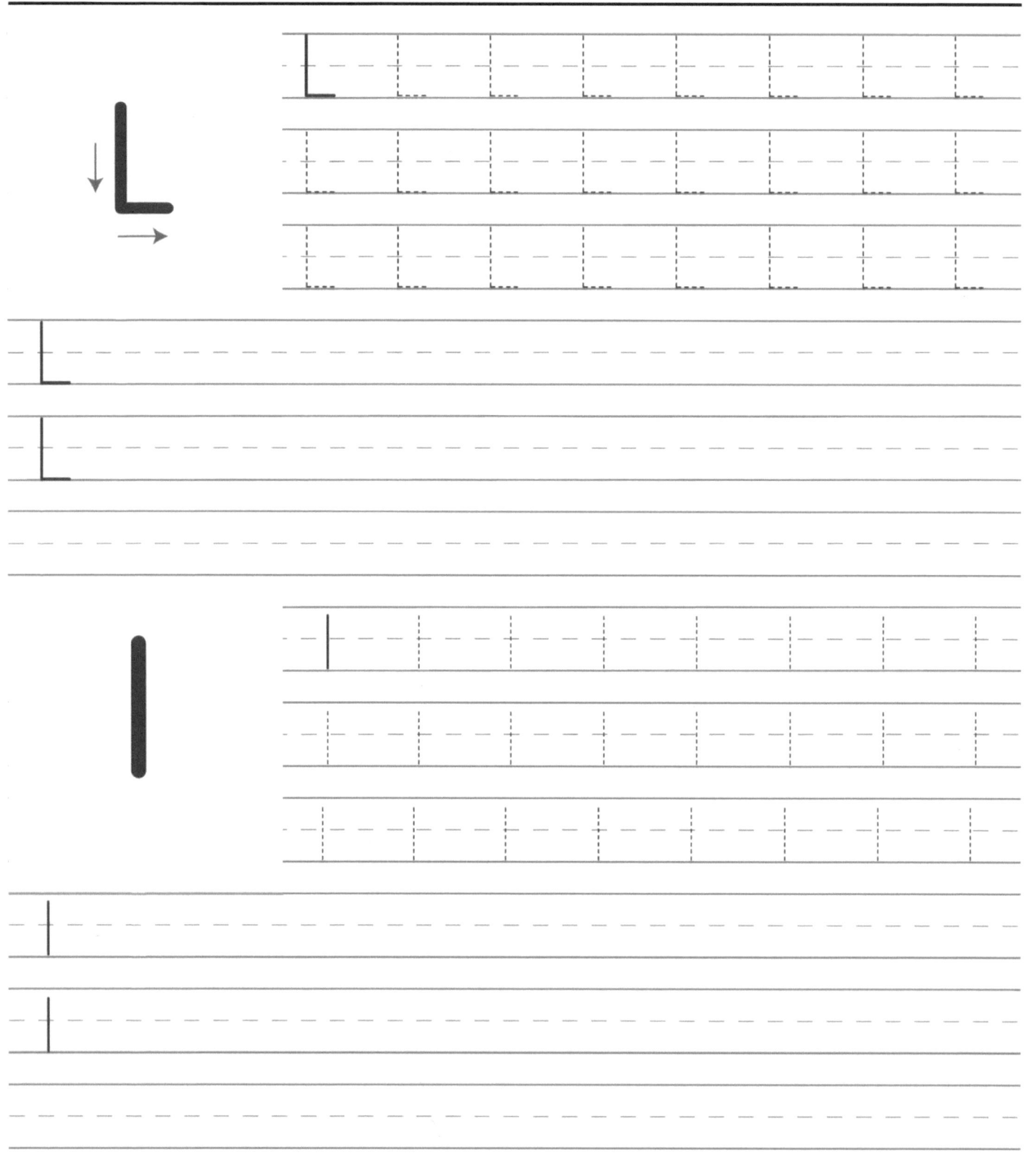

Mm

Oo

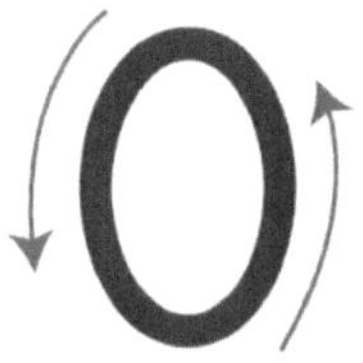

Pp

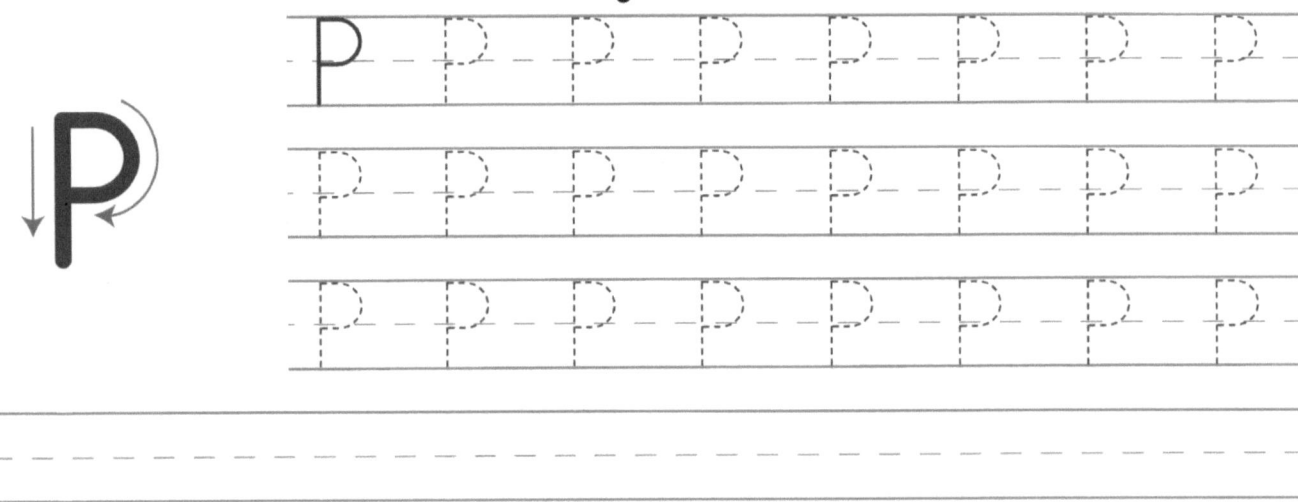

Qq

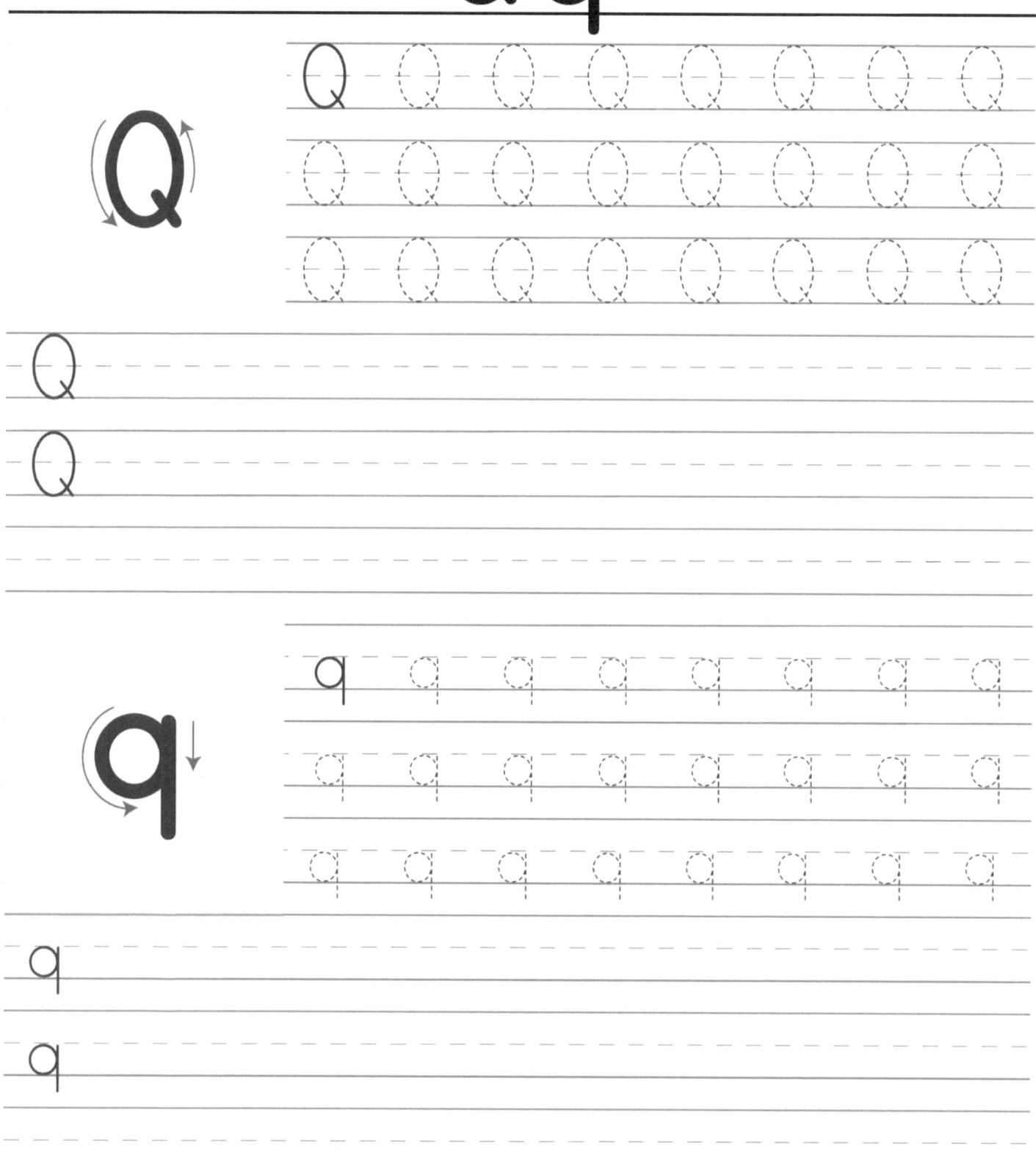

Rr

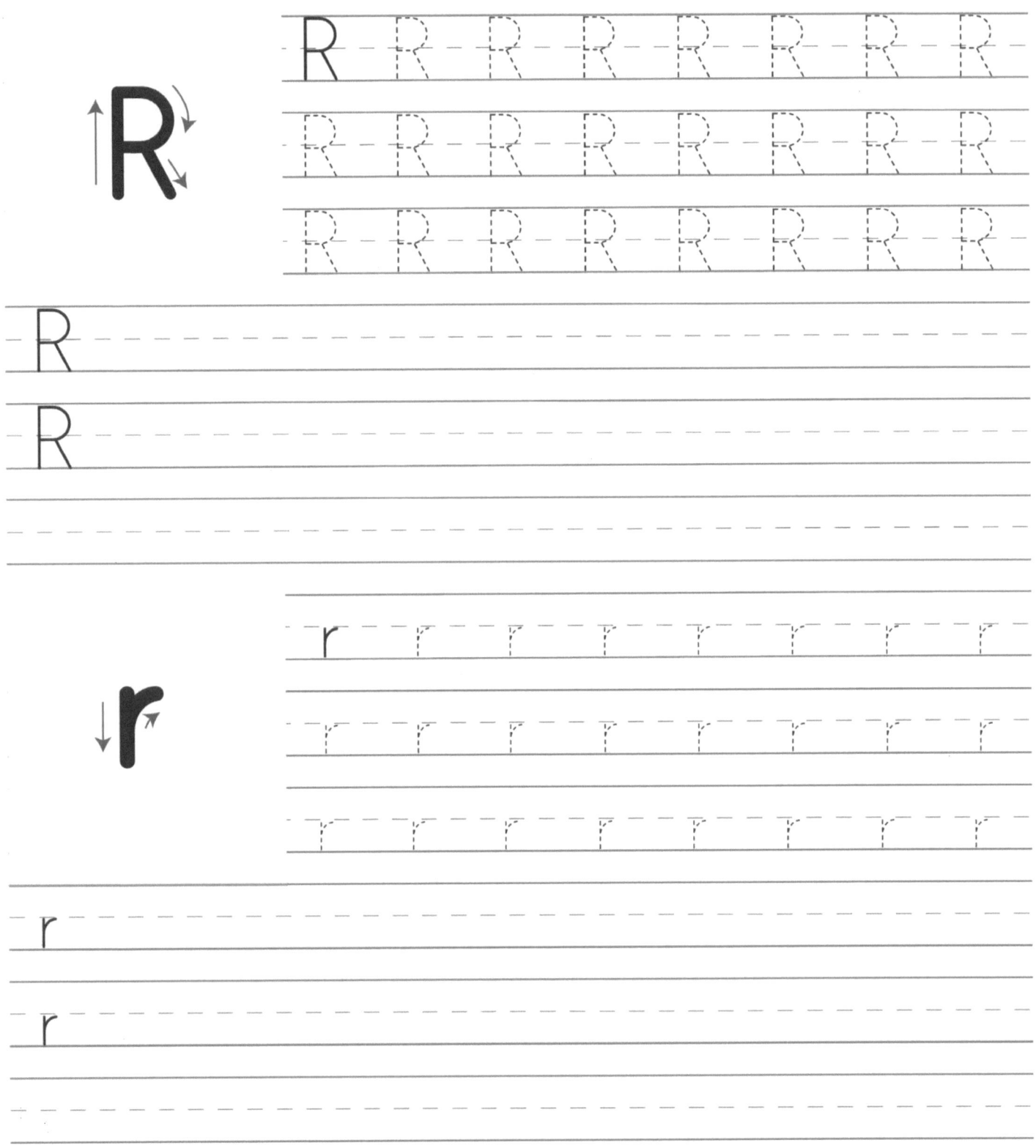

Ss

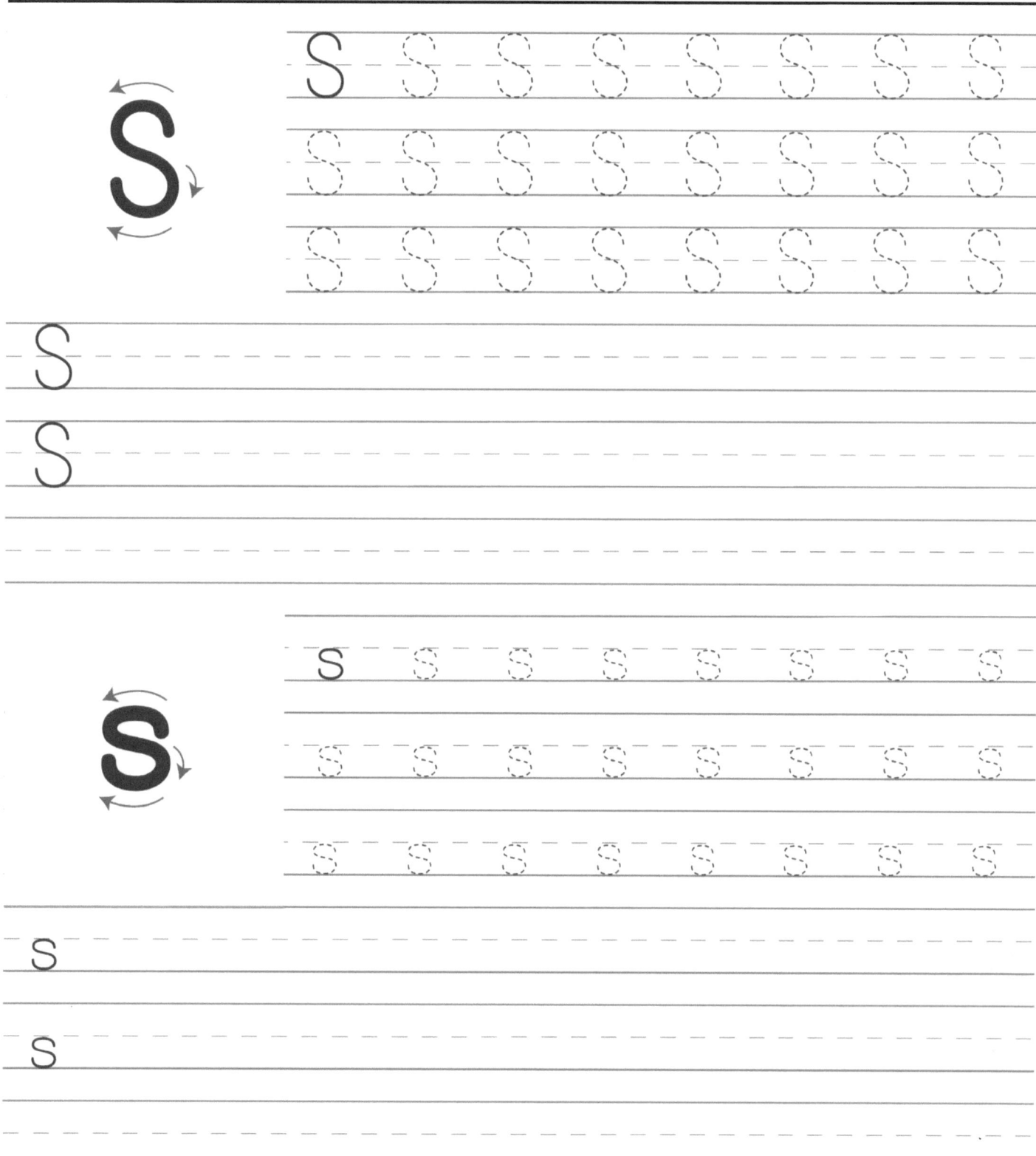

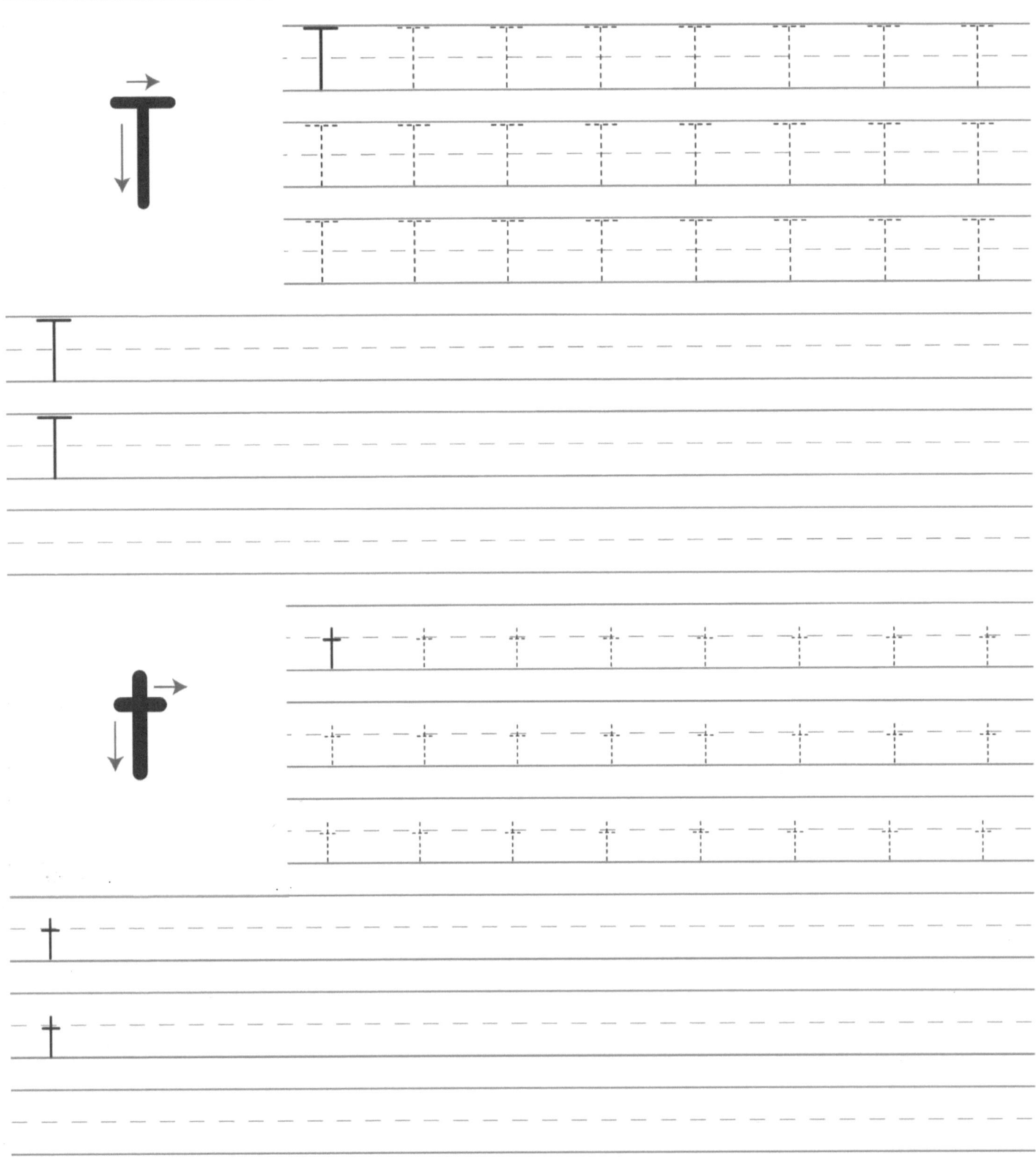

V v

W w

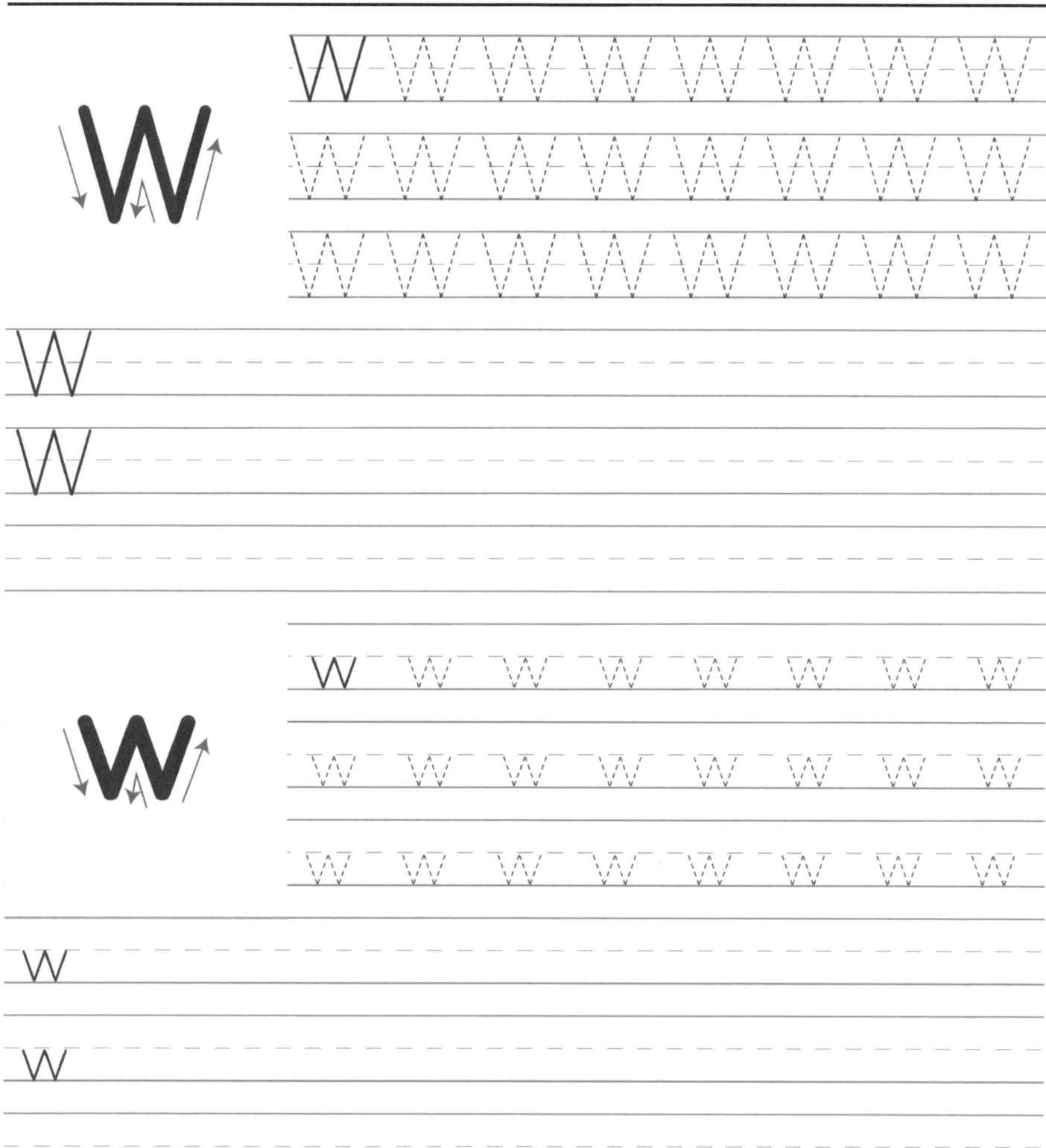

Xx

Yy

Y

Y Y Y Y Y Y Y Y

Y Y Y Y Y Y Y Y

Y Y Y Y Y Y Y Y

Y

Y

y

y y y y y y y y

y y y y y y y y

y y y y y y y y

y

y

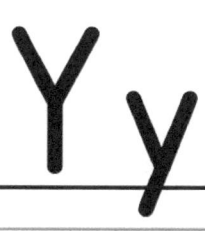

Zz

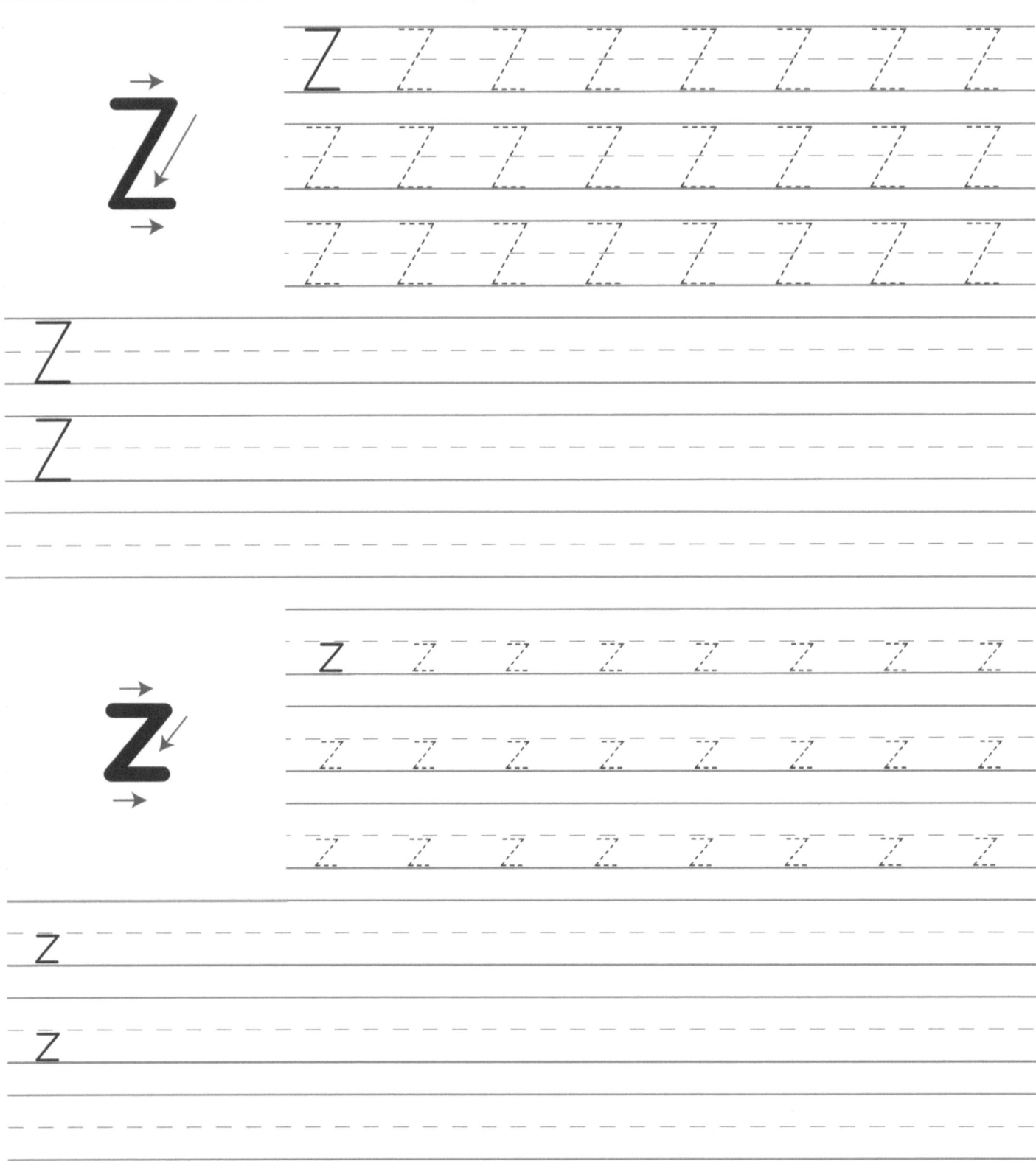

SILLY ANIMAL FACTS AHEAD!

Silly Animal Facts!

Dolphins sleep with one eye open!

Your Turn!

Picture It!

Check Your Work!
- ○ Capitalization
- ○ Finger Spacing
- ○ Punctuation

✓

Silly Animal Facts!

Octopuses have three hearts.

Your Turn!

Picture It!

Check Your Work!
- ○ Capitalization
- ○ Finger Spacing
- ○ Punctuation

✓

Silly Animal Facts!

Butterflies taste with their feet.

Your Turn!

Picture It!

Check Your Work!
- ○ Capitalization
- ○ Finger Spacing
- ○ Punctuation

✓

Silly Animal Facts!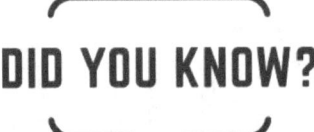

Cows have best friends and get stressed when separated.

Your Turn!

Picture It!

Check Your Work!
- ○ Capitalization
- ○ Finger Spacing
- ○ Punctuation

Silly Animal Facts!

A snail can sleep for three years.

Your Turn!

Picture It!

Check Your Work!
- ○ Capitalization
- ○ Finger Spacing
- ○ Punctuation

✓

Silly Animal Facts!

Kangaroos can't walk backwards.

Your Turn!

Picture It!

Check Your Work!
- ○ Capitalization
- ○ Finger Spacing
- ○ Punctuation

✓

Silly Animal Facts!

Elephants are the only animals that can't jump.

Your Turn!

Picture It!

Check Your Work!
✓
- ○ Capitalization
- ○ Finger Spacing
- ○ Punctuation

Silly Animal Facts!

A rhino's horn is made of hair.

Your Turn!

Picture It!

Check Your Work!
- ○ Capitalization
- ○ Finger Spacing
- ○ Punctuation

Silly Animal Facts!

Frogs can't swallow with their eyes open.

Your Turn!

Picture It!

Check Your Work!
- ○ Capitalization
- ○ Finger Spacing
- ○ Punctuation

✓

Silly Animal Facts!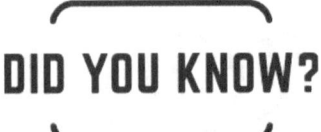

Penguins laugh when they're tickled.

Your Turn!

Picture It!

Check Your Work!
- ◯ Capitalization
- ◯ Finger Spacing
- ◯ Punctuation

Silly Animal Facts!  DID YOU KNOW?

Giraffes have the same number of neck bones as humans.

Your Turn!

Picture It!

Check Your Work!
✓
- ○ Capitalization
- ○ Finger Spacing
- ○ Punctuation

Silly Animal Facts!

Seahorses mate for life and dance every morning.

Your Turn!

Picture It!

Check Your Work!
- ○ Capitalization
- ○ Finger Spacing
- ○ Punctuation

Silly Animal Facts!

Zebras' stripes are unique, like fingerprints.

Your Turn!

Picture It!

Check Your Work!
- ○ Capitalization
- ○ Finger Spacing
- ○ Punctuation

✓

Silly Animal Facts!

Hippos produce pink milk.

Your Turn!

Picture It!

Check Your Work!
- ○ Capitalization
- ○ Finger Spacing
- ○ Punctuation

Silly Animal Facts!

Ostriches have the largest eyes of any land animal.

Your Turn!

Picture It!

Check Your Work!
- ○ Capitalization
- ○ Finger Spacing
- ○ Punctuation

✓

Silly Animal Facts!

Sloths only poop once a week.

Your Turn!

Picture It!

Check Your Work!
- ○ Capitalization
- ○ Finger Spacing
- ○ Punctuation

✓

Silly Animal Facts!

Bees can remember human faces.

Your Turn!

Picture It!

Check Your Work!
- ○ Capitalization
- ○ Finger Spacing
- ○ Punctuation

✓

Silly Animal Facts!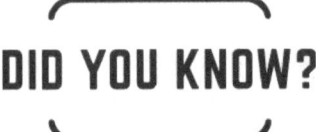

Koalas sleep up to 22 hours a day.

Your Turn!

Picture It!

Check Your Work!
- ○ Capitalization
- ○ Finger Spacing
- ○ Punctuation

✓

Silly Animal Facts!  DID YOU KNOW?

Turtles can breathe through their butts.

Your Turn!

Picture It!

Check Your Work!
✓
- ○ Capitalization
- ○ Finger Spacing
- ○ Punctuation

Silly Animal Facts!

Hummingbirds fly backwards.

Your Turn!

Picture It!

Check Your Work!
✓
- ○ Capitalization
- ○ Finger Spacing
- ○ Punctuation

Silly Animal Facts!

Crocodiles can't stick out their tongues.

Your Turn!

Picture It!

Check Your Work!
- ○ Capitalization
- ○ Finger Spacing
- ○ Punctuation

✓

Silly Animal Facts!

Sharks have been around longer than trees.

Your Turn!

Picture It!

Check Your Work!
- ○ Capitalization
- ○ Finger Spacing
- ○ Punctuation

Silly Animal Facts!

Ants never sleep.

Your Turn!

Picture It!

Check Your Work!
- ○ Capitalization
- ○ Finger Spacing
- ○ Punctuation

✓

Silly Animal Facts!

Parrots can mimic many sounds, even human speech.

Your Turn!

Picture It!

Check Your Work!
- ○ Capitalization
- ○ Finger Spacing
- ○ Punctuation

✓

Silly Animal Facts!

Goats have rectangular pupils.

Your Turn!

Picture It!

Check Your Work!
- ○ Capitalization
- ○ Finger Spacing
- ○ Punctuation

✓

Silly Animal Facts!

Cats have a third eyelid.

Your Turn!

Picture It!

Check Your Work!
- ○ Capitalization
- ○ Finger Spacing
- ○ Punctuation

✓

Silly Animal Facts!

Dogs' nose prints are as unique as human fingerprints.

Your Turn!

Picture It!

Check Your Work!
- ☐ Capitalization
- ☐ Finger Spacing
- ☐ Punctuation

✓

Silly Animal Facts!

Mice sing like birds, but we can't hear them.

Your Turn!

Picture It!

Check Your Work!
- ○ Capitalization
- ○ Finger Spacing
- ○ Punctuation

Silly Animal Facts!

Starfish don't have a brain.

Your Turn!

Picture It!

Check Your Work!
- ☐ Capitalization
- ☐ Finger Spacing
- ☐ Punctuation

✓

Silly Animal Facts!

A bat can eat up to 1,000 insects per hour.

Your Turn!

Picture It!

Check Your Work!
- ○ Capitalization
- ○ Finger Spacing
- ○ Punctuation

✓

Silly Animal Facts!

Camels have three eyelids to protect against sand.

Your Turn!

Picture It!

Check Your Work!
✓
- ○ Capitalization
- ○ Finger Spacing
- ○ Punctuation

Silly Animal Facts!

The tongue of a blue whale weighs as much as an elephant.

Your Turn!

Picture It!

Check Your Work!
- ○ Capitalization
- ○ Finger Spacing
- ○ Punctuation

✓

Silly Animal Facts!

Chameleons change color to express their mood.

Your Turn!

Picture It!

Check Your Work!
- ☐ Capitalization
- ☐ Finger Spacing
- ☐ Punctuation

✓

Silly Animal Facts!

Peacocks can grow up to thirteen feet in length.

Your Turn!

Picture It!

Check Your Work!
- ☐ Capitalization
- ☐ Finger Spacing
- ☐ Punctuation

✓

Silly Animal Facts!

Armadillos have bulletproof shells.

Your Turn!

Picture It!

Check Your Work!
- ○ Capitalization
- ○ Finger Spacing
- ○ Punctuation

✓

Silly Animal Facts!

An octopus has blue blood.

Your Turn!

Picture It!

Check Your Work!
- ○ Capitalization
- ○ Finger Spacing
- ○ Punctuation

Silly Animal Facts!

Lobsters taste with their legs.

Your Turn!

Picture It!

Check Your Work!
- ○ Capitalization
- ○ Finger Spacing
- ○ Punctuation

✓

Silly Animal Facts!

Dragonflies have six legs but can't walk.

Your Turn!

Picture It!

Check Your Work!
- ○ Capitalization
- ○ Finger Spacing
- ○ Punctuation

✓

Silly Animal Facts!

Wombat poop is cube-shaped.

Your Turn!

Picture It!

Check Your Work!
- ○ Capitalization
- ○ Finger Spacing
- ○ Punctuation

✓

Silly Animal Facts!

Goldfish can see both infrared and ultraviolet light.

Your Turn!

Picture It!

Check Your Work!
- ○ Capitalization
- ○ Finger Spacing
- ○ Punctuation

✓

Silly Animal Facts!

Pigs are among the smartest domestic animals.

Your Turn!

Picture It!

Check Your Work!
- ○ Capitalization
- ○ Finger Spacing
- ○ Punctuation

✓

Silly Animal Facts!

Deer have no gall bladders.

Your Turn!

Picture It!

Check Your Work!
- ○ Capitalization
- ○ Finger Spacing
- ○ Punctuation

✓

Silly Animal Facts!

Male seahorses give birth to their young.

Your Turn!

Picture It!

Check Your Work!
- ○ Capitalization
- ○ Finger Spacing
- ○ Punctuation

✓

Silly Animal Facts!

Cheetahs can't roar, they meow like house cats.

Your Turn!

Picture It!

Check Your Work!
- ○ Capitalization
- ○ Finger Spacing
- ○ Punctuation

✓

Silly Animal Facts!

Frogs absorb water through their skin.

Your Turn!

Picture It!

Check Your Work!
- ○ Capitalization
- ○ Finger Spacing
- ○ Punctuation

✓

Silly Animal Facts!

Spiders have blue blood.

Your Turn!

Picture It!

Check Your Work!
- ○ Capitalization
- ○ Finger Spacing
- ○ Punctuation

✓

Silly Animal Facts!

Albatrosses can sleep while flying.

Your Turn!

Picture It!

Check Your Work!
- ☐ Capitalization
- ☐ Finger Spacing
- ☐ Punctuation

✓

Silly Animal Facts!

Axolotls can regenerate lost body parts.

Your Turn!

Picture It!

Check Your Work!
- ○ Capitalization
- ○ Finger Spacing
- ○ Punctuation

Silly Animal Facts!

Owls don't have eyeballs, they have eye tubes.

Your Turn!

Picture It!

Check Your Work!
- ○ Capitalization
- ○ Finger Spacing
- ○ Punctuation

✓

Silly Animal Facts!

Fireflies aren't flies, they're beetles.

Your Turn!

Picture It!

Check Your Work!
- ○ Capitalization
- ○ Finger Spacing
- ○ Punctuation

✓

Silly Animal Facts!

A single honeybee will produce only about 1/12th teaspoon of honey in its lifetime.

Your Turn!

Picture It!

Check Your Work!
- ○ Capitalization
- ○ Finger Spacing
- ○ Punctuation

✓

Silly Animal Facts!

Snakes can help predict earthquakes.

Your Turn!

Picture It!

Check Your Work!
- ○ Capitalization
- ○ Finger Spacing
- ○ Punctuation

✓

Silly Animal Facts!

Bats always turn left when exiting a cave.

Your Turn!

Picture It!

Check Your Work!
- ○ Capitalization
- ○ Finger Spacing
- ○ Punctuation

✓

Silly Animal Facts!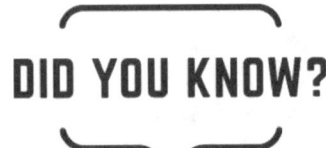

Elephants can hear with their feet.

Your Turn!

Picture It!

Check Your Work!
- ○ Capitalization
- ○ Finger Spacing
- ○ Punctuation

✓

Silly Animal Facts!

Giraffes have purple tongues to prevent sunburn.

Your Turn!

Picture It!

Check Your Work!
- ☐ Capitalization
- ☐ Finger Spacing
- ☐ Punctuation

✓

Silly Animal Facts!

The Basenji dog is the only dog breed that can't bark.

Your Turn!

Picture It!

Check Your Work!
- ○ Capitalization
- ○ Finger Spacing
- ○ Punctuation

✓

Silly Animal Facts!

Baby sharks are born with teeth and ready to swim.

Your Turn!

Picture It!

Check Your Work!
- ○ Capitalization
- ○ Finger Spacing
- ○ Punctuation

✓

Silly Animal Facts!

Some turtles can live to be over 100 years old.

Your Turn!

Picture It!

Check Your Work!
- ○ Capitalization
- ○ Finger Spacing
- ○ Punctuation

✓

Silly Animal Facts!

Jellyfish have been around longer than dinosaurs.

Your Turn!

Picture It!

Check Your Work!
- ○ Capitalization
- ○ Finger Spacing
- ○ Punctuation

✓

Silly Animal Facts!

A baby puffin is called a "puffling."

Your Turn!

Picture It!

Check Your Work!
- ○ Capitalization
- ○ Finger Spacing
- ○ Punctuation

Silly Animal Facts!

Male pandas do handstands to mark trees.

Your Turn!

Picture It!

Check Your Work!
- ○ Capitalization
- ○ Finger Spacing
- ○ Punctuation

✓

Silly Animal Facts!

An elephant's trunk has more than 40,000 muscles.

Your Turn!

Picture It!

Check Your Work!
- ○ Capitalization
- ○ Finger Spacing
- ○ Punctuation

✓

Silly Animal Facts!

Hummingbirds weigh less than a penny.

Your Turn!

Picture It!

Check Your Work!
- ○ Capitalization
- ○ Finger Spacing
- ○ Punctuation

✓

Silly Animal Facts!

The fingerprints of koalas are so similar to humans that they can confuse crime scene evidence.

Your Turn!

Picture It!

Check Your Work!
- ○ Capitalization
- ○ Finger Spacing
- ○ Punctuation

✓

Silly Animal Facts!

Some frogs can freeze without dying.

Your Turn!

Picture It!

Check Your Work!
- ○ Capitalization
- ○ Finger Spacing
- ○ Punctuation

✓

Silly Animal Facts!

The heart of a shrimp is located in its head.

Your Turn!

Picture It!

Check Your Work!
- ○ Capitalization
- ○ Finger Spacing
- ○ Punctuation

✓

Silly Animal Facts!

Sloths can turn their heads almost 360 degrees.

Your Turn!

Picture It!

Check Your Work!
- ○ Capitalization
- ○ Finger Spacing
- ○ Punctuation

✓

Silly Animal Facts!

Anteaters don't have teeth.

Your Turn!

Picture It!

Check Your Work!
- ○ Capitalization
- ○ Finger Spacing
- ○ Punctuation

Silly Animal Facts!

The world's smallest mammal is the bumblebee bat.

Your Turn!

Picture It!

Check Your Work!
- ◯ Capitalization
- ◯ Finger Spacing
- ◯ Punctuation

✓

Silly Animal Facts!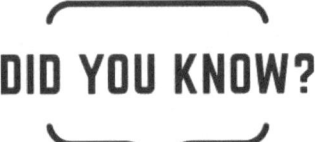

The color of a hen's earlobe can tell you the color of the egg she will lay.

Your Turn!

Picture It!

Check Your Work!
- ○ Capitalization
- ○ Finger Spacing
- ○ Punctuation

Silly Animal Facts!

Flamingos are born with gray feathers.

Your Turn!

Picture It!

Check Your Work!
- ○ Capitalization
- ○ Finger Spacing
- ○ Punctuation

✓

Silly Animal Facts!

The male platypus has a venomous spur on its hind foot.

Your Turn!

Picture It!

Check Your Work!
- ○ Capitalization
- ○ Finger Spacing
- ○ Punctuation

✓

Silly Animal Facts!

Parrotfish sleep in a bubble of their own mucus.

Your Turn!

Picture It!

Check Your Work!
- ○ Capitalization
- ○ Finger Spacing
- ○ Punctuation

Silly Animal Facts!

Octopuses have nine brains.

Your Turn!

Picture It!

Check Your Work!
- ○ Capitalization
- ○ Finger Spacing
- ○ Punctuation

✓

Silly Animal Facts!

The longest recorded flight of a chicken is thirteen seconds.

Your Turn!

Picture It!

Check Your Work!
- ○ Capitalization
- ○ Finger Spacing
- ○ Punctuation

✓

Silly Animal Facts!

Baby echidnas are called "puggles."

Your Turn!

Picture It!

Check Your Work!
- ○ Capitalization
- ○ Finger Spacing
- ○ Punctuation

✓

Silly Animal Facts!

Moths have no stomach.

Your Turn!

Picture It!

Check Your Work!
- ○ Capitalization
- ○ Finger Spacing
- ○ Punctuation

✓

Silly Animal Facts!

Turkeys can blush.

Your Turn!

Picture It!

Check Your Work!
- ☐ Capitalization
- ☐ Finger Spacing
- ☐ Punctuation

✓

Silly Animal Facts!

The mantis shrimp has the world's fastest punch.

Your Turn!

Picture It!

Check Your Work!
- ☐ Capitalization
- ☐ Finger Spacing
- ☐ Punctuation

Silly Animal Facts!

Pigeons can do math at the level of human preschoolers.

Your Turn!

Picture It!

Check Your Work!
- ○ Capitalization
- ○ Finger Spacing
- ○ Punctuation

Silly Animal Facts!

Lobsters have teeth in their stomachs.

Your Turn!

Picture It!

Check Your Work!
- ○ Capitalization
- ○ Finger Spacing
- ○ Punctuation

✓

Silly Animal Facts!

The male narwhal's tusk is actually an elongated tooth.

Your Turn!

Picture It!

Check Your Work!
- ○ Capitalization
- ○ Finger Spacing
- ○ Punctuation

✓

Silly Animal Facts!

Reindeer's eyes change color with the seasons.

Your Turn!

Picture It!

Check Your Work!
- ☐ Capitalization
- ☐ Finger Spacing
- ☐ Punctuation

✓

Silly Animal Facts!

Platypuses glow under ultraviolet light.

Your Turn!

Picture It!

Check Your Work!
- ◯ Capitalization
- ◯ Finger Spacing
- ◯ Punctuation

✓

Silly Animal Facts!

Dung beetles navigate by the stars.

Your Turn!

Picture It!

Check Your Work!
- ○ Capitalization
- ○ Finger Spacing
- ○ Punctuation

✓

Silly Animal Facts!

Some species of earthworms can have up to ten hearts.

Your Turn!

Picture It!

Check Your Work!
- ○ Capitalization
- ○ Finger Spacing
- ○ Punctuation

✓

Silly Animal Facts!

The average chicken can run up to nine mph.

Your Turn!

Picture It!

Check Your Work!
- ○ Capitalization
- ○ Finger Spacing
- ○ Punctuation

✓

Silly Animal Facts!

An ostrich's eye is bigger than its brain.

Your Turn!

Picture It!

Check Your Work!
- ○ Capitalization
- ○ Finger Spacing
- ○ Punctuation

✓

Silly Animal Facts!

There's a jellyfish species that can age backward.

Your Turn!

Picture It!

Check Your Work!
- ○ Capitalization
- ○ Finger Spacing
- ○ Punctuation

✓

Silly Animal Facts!

The sailfish is the fastest fish in the ocean.

Your Turn!

Picture It!

Check Your Work!
✓
- ○ Capitalization
- ○ Finger Spacing
- ○ Punctuation

Silly Animal Facts!

Vampire bats share their food with less fortunate bats.

Your Turn!

Picture It!

Check Your Work!
- ○ Capitalization
- ○ Finger Spacing
- ○ Punctuation

✓

Silly Animal Facts!

Seahorses can move their eyes independently.

Your Turn!

Picture It!

Check Your Work!
- ○ Capitalization
- ○ Finger Spacing
- ○ Punctuation

✓

Silly Animal Facts!

The only mammal capable of true flight is the bat.

Your Turn!

Picture It!

Check Your Work!
- ○ Capitalization
- ○ Finger Spacing
- ○ Punctuation

✓

Silly Animal Facts!

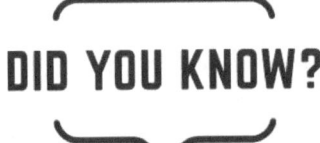

The longest recorded lifespan of a slug is six years.

Your Turn!

Picture It!

Check Your Work!
- ○ Capitalization
- ○ Finger Spacing
- ○ Punctuation

✓

Silly Animal Facts!

The world's smallest bird is the bee hummingbird.

Your Turn!

Picture It!

Check Your Work!
- ○ Capitalization
- ○ Finger Spacing
- ○ Punctuation

✓

Silly Animal Facts!

The blood of horseshoe crabs is blue.

Your Turn!

Picture It!

Check Your Work!
- ○ Capitalization
- ○ Finger Spacing
- ○ Punctuation

✓

Silly Animal Facts!

DID YOU KNOW?

Elephants can paint using their trunks.

Your Turn!

Picture It!

Check Your Work!
- ○ Capitalization
- ○ Finger Spacing
- ○ Punctuation

✓

Silly Animal Facts!

A cat's whiskers are roughly as wide as its body.

Your Turn!

Picture It!

Check Your Work!
- ○ Capitalization
- ○ Finger Spacing
- ○ Punctuation

✓

Silly Animal Facts!

Gorillas can catch human colds and other illnesses.

Your Turn!

Picture It!

Check Your Work!
✓
- ○ Capitalization
- ○ Finger Spacing
- ○ Punctuation

Silly Animal Facts!

A single elephant tooth can weigh over 9 pounds.

Your Turn!

Picture It!

Check Your Work!
- ○ Capitalization
- ○ Finger Spacing
- ○ Punctuation

✓

THANK YOU!

If you enjoyed this book, please consider leaving a review on Amazon. It will help us reach more people.

We invite you to check out our other books. We offer everything from coloring and activity books to popular fiction and short stories!

WANT MORE KID APPROVED BOOKS?

Scan the QR code to see our other books on Amazon!

www.amazon.com/author/clawandson

Made in United States
Troutdale, OR
06/20/2024

20692671R00077